52

The Age of

New Life

in

Jesus

Gracefully Broken

CAROLVET WILLHITE-TUMBS

WESTBOW
PRESS®
A DIVISION OF THOMAS NELSON
& ZONDERVAN

WestBow Press books may be ordered through booksellers or by contacting:

WestBow Press
A Division of Thomas Nelson & Zondervan
1663 Liberty Drive
Bloomington, IN 47403
www.westbowpress.com
844-714-3454

Scripture taken from the King James Version of the Bible.

ISBN: 978-1-6642-0803-2 (sc)
ISBN: 978-1-6642-0804-9 (e)

Print information available on the last page.

WestBow Press rev. date: 10/29/2020

Contents

Dedication

I give all glory and honor to God the Father and his Son Jesus for life. This story could not be told if it were not for love, grace, and mercy from Abba, my Father.

This book is dedicated to my mom,
Barbara J. Willhite (1947–2016).

MOM

Thank you to my beloved siblings, friends, and family who stood by my side as I journeyed through a world of changes. Most of all, I want to give a special thanks to my son, D. He has been there through it all; he never left my side. I know it was not easy on him or his sister. My prayer partner Hope Campbell prayed me through many nights. If not for this woman of God, I do not know how I would have made it. To my beloved sister in Christ and best friend Brenda Plummer and to my daughter (Shavanna) Shay—thank you for your understanding during this struggle. We had some hard times, but we made it through as a family. I love you and Dstarr. Thank you to Evangelist Kim of Original Church of God and so many others who showed me the love of Christ. Thank you all for your support and love.

Preface

Let me say this first: I know I am called to the office of a prophet. I operated in the gift but got scared because I did not understand who I truly was and tried not to operate in the gift. I began to think I was weird because things I said happened. I would dream of numbers and play them in the lottery. Sometimes I would win, and sometimes I would not. I have experienced trancelike states. I have dreamed things as they were happening at that very moment. One person told me to not ever tell him anything again. That person was my first love. God had instructed me to tell him something, and it came to pass, word for word—and it scared me. I thought I spoke this upon him; I had no idea at that time that I was giving him a word of prophecy.

Satan has been trying to kill me since I was age two. At the time of writing this book, I was fifty-two years old; I am now fifty-four years of age. Satan desires to sift me as wheat, but I have taken a stand on God's Word in my life, and to see the beauty of it unfold is amazing and mind-blowing. As children of God, we will find ourselves in unpleasant situations and conditions. Sometimes this is by our own doing, and other times, it is because of someone else's actions. I know I was put in this situation by the devil because he had a plan that was meant for my destruction, but my God said, "No!" God said that I would not die but would live to declare the works of the Lord. Something about this attack on my life pushed me into a new place in God. I understand now more than ever that I must walk in the calling God has placed on my life. The devil knows the power and authority of Jesus Christ. He does not want us to know that power.

The Beginning

February 2, 2018 began a new chapter in my life. I had no idea my world was about to take a major turn and that everything that can be shaken was being shaken. While I was in the hospital, I heard the Holy Spirit say, "Write a book about this." The Holy Spirit said to title the book *Fifty-Two: The Age of New Life in Jesus*. It was a Friday. I purchased lunch at work—tilapia with wild rice and broccoli. Well, the tilapia got me sick. I tasted a piece of the fish, and it tasted funny to me. I thought it was me because it was the first time I had it breaded. I ate some of the rice and broccoli, tried the fish again, and had the same response, so I did not eat any more of it.

I worked the rest of my shift but started to feel sick to my stomach about half an hour after work. Again, I did not think much of it. I figured it was because I did not eat the lunch. Well, I went through the weekend getting worse; then I started feeling like I had the flu, so I took some flu medication. Things did not get any better. I finally made it to Wednesday. By then, I had horrific stomach pain, so I had my son take me to the local ER after taking care of some business. They got me stable enough to go home but told me to follow up with my primary doctor as soon as possible. I visited my doctor that Saturday, February 10, 2018. She had me hospitalized that day, not knowing what was wrong or what had happened to me.

After several days of blood tests and cultures, I was finally diagnosed with a bacterial infection known as H-pylori. This infection could have killed me. It attacked my immune system and caused it to malfunction. My immune system began to attack my organs because it was off balance. It thought the organs were broken and needed to be repaired.

Doctors told me that my heart, lungs, and kidneys were affected by this. The attending doctor said the treatment would need to be aggressive. Once they knew what the problem was, they wanted to combat the infection the same way it attacked my body, which was aggressively. Doctors said I had to have four chemo treatments for this infection because it had attacked the immune system. During this time in the hospital, I had dreams and visions. I also heard the Holy Spirit speak.

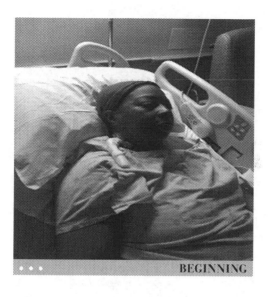

BEGINNING

Dream 1: February 16, 2018

It was dark outside in the dream. I was helping people get to safety by guiding them to an old fire station. I was telling the people that if they wanted to be saved, they should go into the building. The building was illuminated as if it were a guiding light. As I was showing people where to go, I heard in my spirit that a storm was coming, and the sky was lighting up. I woke from the dream at this point.

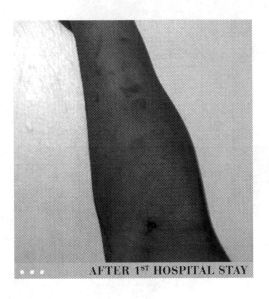

AFTER 1ST HOSPITAL STAY

Dream 2: February 20, 2018

I dreamed that a girlfriend of mine was being held hostage by some guy looking for money. He made her call people to get money or he would kill her. In this dream, I was in the hospital. I could hear the guy on the phone. I called for the nurse in the dream and asked her to call the police. Somehow, in the dream, the police were able to find out where he was holding my friend and saved her. The guy was arrested; they found them in an apartment that was across from my hospital room. As they were bringing this guy out, he looked me in the face and told me he was putting a hit out on my life. Then I woke from the dream.

On February 27, 2018, I woke up praising God and saying, "Only you know why I was chosen to go through what seems to be the same thing my mother went through." I found myself saying, "I accept." At some point, my hospital room turned completely black. I began to ask, "God, what is this? What is happening?" I then began to tell the Lord that it could not be my time to die. There were prophecies that had been spoken over my life that had not come to pass yet. At that very moment, the room suddenly turned all white. I was in the hospital until March 1, 2018 but ended up right back in the hospital on March 5, 2018.

The Middle

By March 5, 2018, I was back in the hospital for another two weeks, diagnosed with heart failure. During my second stay in the hospital, the Holy Spirit really ministered to me. I was broken by what was happening to me and did not understand what was going on. The doctors were saying so many different things that everything was overwhelming. I asked God what happened to me. I felt like the rug had been pulled from up under my feet, and my world came to a halt. I kept seeing visions of myself in a black box with no way out.

While in that hospital bed, I began to see the room turn black. I started praying and crying out to God. I continued to cry out to God, calling on the name of Jesus to help me. I told him, "I do not believe you brought me this far to leave me. There were prophecies spoken to me that have not come to pass. It cannot be my time." At that very moment, the room turned completely white. I knew then that the life I once knew was no more.

I began to say to the Lord whatever this is, take me through this, Lord, for your glory. I heard in my spirit, *Because you resisted the enemy, elevation has come, and now you truly can understand the pain your mother was in and went through.* The Holy Spirit said that I was walking in my mother's shoes. The illness that hit me took me through the same health issues that my mother went through without me having to go through dialysis. On March 5, 2018, my doctors called to tell me that I need to get to the ER and that I would be readmitted. Some blood work came back indicating heart failure. The Spirit of the Lord said to me, "Keep quiet. You are at a fork in the road. Choose this day whom you will truly serve."

During this stay, I had an experience with one of the nurses. I was doing well until that nurse came on shift. I did not know what happened, but everything changed, and I started to become disoriented. Some of my family came to visit that day, but when they left, the attack escalated, and the war started. My blood pressure fell very low, and all I could hear was the nurse saying, "You are going to ICU."

My response to her was, "What did you do to me?" I told her she was evil; this did not happen to me until she came on shift. As that day went on, I was getting worse. I began to hear the Holy Spirit tell me to say no whenever that nurse or PCT asked me if I needed anything for pain, so I did just that. Every time either one entered the room after that, my response to any of their questions was a *no*, just as the Holy Spirit said. I had to use a bedside toilet during this time. At some point, I was left to sit there in my waste. But by the morning, God turned it all around. My blood pressure recovered, and I did not end up in ICU.

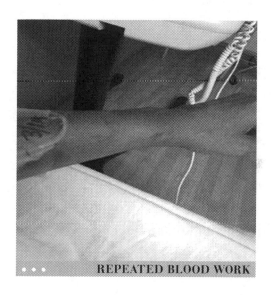

REPEATED BLOOD WORK

Second Hospital Stay

I was discharged again on March 22, 2018 by demand. I needed to get home and worship, so I told the doctors I could recover at home, and I was persistent about it. They finally agreed to let me go home. I went home and did just that, and it allowed me the opportunity to rebuild my relationship with God. The next Saturday, I had a follow-up appointment with a doctor. I heard by way of the Spirit, "She is going to try to turn the lights on you." I was spiritually attacked during that visit. That doctor came in the room and literally cut the lights out. I asked why she did that. She said, "Oh, I thought the light bothered your eyes." My spirit left my body while she spoke. I do not know what she was saying, but when my spirit came back into my body, it came back with a warning—that God knows everything and will deal with it.

When I got ready to leave that office, I had a lump in my throat. I heard the Spirit say, "Do not swallow; spit it out." I did. That doctor proceeded to call me daily for about two weeks all hours of the day to see how I was doing. I kept my appointments and was recovering well. I was able to return to work by April 23, 2018. I worked four hours a day, five days a week. I worked all the way up to July 3, 2018 before another attack came upon me. On a Monday, I got home from work and suddenly got sick. I started throwing up and having diarrhea. I also felt severe pain. I had to go to the ER; they got me fixed up, stabilized me, and sent me home.

Things went well until the end of the month. During most of this time, I was not able to eat. I lost my taste for food. Sweets did not taste like sweets, and salt did not have a taste. I was on a low-fiber diet. It was hard to adjust my eating because of my taste buds. I had no taste buds. I went from a size eighteen or twenty to an eight or ten in pants. My weight dropped from about 213 pounds to 147 pounds. I no longer had any muscle tone. It was nice to see but difficult to believe how my whole world suddenly changed. God says in his Word that all things are working together for my good because I love God, and I am called according to his purpose (Romans 8:28). This is the scripture that helped to pull and guide me through the tribulation of what was happening in my life.

3

CHAPTER

Declaring Healing
in Jesus's Name

On July 30, 2018, I again suddenly got sick after coming home from working just four hours. I went to the ER, and they sent me home, but within the hour, I was back at the ER because I was in so much pain. I was throwing up and had to go right back. While there the second time in one day, I had a mild heart attack. I had to be put in an induced coma. I started to come to by that Thursday, August 2, 2018. By Friday, August 3, 2018, I came to but could not believe what was happening to me. I was discharged on August 5, 2018.

On August 9, the Holy Spirit spoke and told me I had cancer, I would be healed, and it would never come back. I was at home in worship when he said it. Then I was right back in the hospital by the tenth of August. I was released on August 14, 2018. August of 2018 was a time of very intense spiritual warfare for my soul. So much blood work and three blood cultures were taken in just a day; it was horrific. In September 2018, I was still getting the results of all the tests that were done. I know my God has healed me in his Son Jesus Christ's name, and I understand that delay does not mean defeat. This is not over yet, and I already have the victory over this affliction.

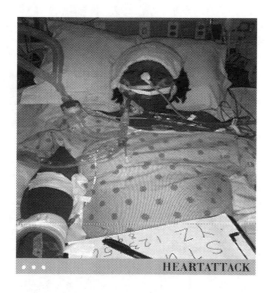

HEARTATTACK

The Wait

The doctors said they were not sure what was wrong with me. They spoke of what could possibly be wrong and wanted me to get a second opinion. I found another doctor to get a second opinion. I had been in prayer, and I needed to see God perform a miracle in my life that was tangible and meaningful to me. That miracle would thrust me into another place in him through my faith. He did just what I asked for, and healing took place in my kitchen. I was barely able to clean my house, but I stood at the sink, washing dishes and listening to my worship music. The Lord began to minister to me. When I went for my next lab work, my lab work looked better.

I was trusting and taking God at his word because it had been proven in my life to be what it says it is (true and living). It can do what it says for God's children. He sent us a comforter in the form of the Holy Spirit so that no matter what we go through here on earth, we can trust God and take him at his word. My only advice is to study the Word of God so that when life's hard times come—and they will—you have something to stand on. If not, it will be easier for the devil and his forces to beat you down to defeat—and in some cases, death. I did end up going back to the local ER twice since I was last released from the hospital. Thanks be to God almighty for keeping me.

On November 6, 2018, doctors diagnosed me with colon cancer. I had a second opinion that was wrong because that doctor diagnosed just off questions—no test or lab work. Well, I went for a third opinion. I told that doctor what was going on in my body. I told him some of what I went through. He ran all kinds of tests. When he had the results, he called me to come into his office. The diagnosis was cancer.

I was still standing and trusting the Word of God. God is not man; he does not lie (Numbers 23:19). He says in his Word that we are healed by the stripes of Jesus. His Word states in Isaiah 53:5 that healing is ours, and with his stripes, we are healed. God spoke through his prophets Michael Haynes and John Veal to confirm my healing.

Doctors wanted to operate as soon as possible. It was the month of December. I refused to be in the hospital at the end of the year after all that I had been through. December 31, 2018, finally arrived, and everything was coming along okay. I was still feeling bad. On the way to church, all of a sudden, I started to get sick. My son was driving; he asked me if he should turn around and take me back home. I said, "No, I will be in the house of God as long as I have breath in this body. I will not end this year 2018 in the hospital." We made it to church. Although I was in much pain, I was in the house of worship, and I blessed the Lord because he allowed me to see and welcome in a new life and year in 2019.

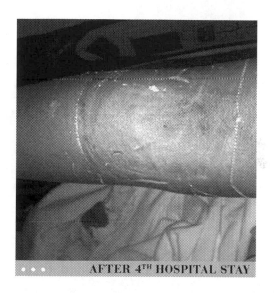

AFTER 4ᵀᴴ HOSPITAL STAY

Proverbs 3:5–6 says, "Trust in the LORD with all thine heart; and lean not unto thine own understanding. In all thy ways acknowledge him, and he shall direct thy paths." This scripture was good meat to my soul because I did not understand anything that was happening to me.

GRADUATION DAY 2018

Through it all, I was able to walk across the stage and get my second degree, although it was a bittersweet moment. My mom was not there to see it. We had made plans prior to her passing. Again, my son was there with me, as was the Holy Spirit. To God be all the glory in Jesus's great and mighty name. As I write this, I am still fighting for my health and my life, but I trust God and take him at his word that I am healed. When this is over, there will be a testimony to glorify God and what he has done. Thank you to my Lord and Savior Jesus Christ.

5

The Surgery and Chemotherapy

Surgery to remove the cancer occurred in February 2019. Now I am in the process of going through chemotherapy. I was told that I will need to do six months of treatments occurring every two weeks. Treatments started in March 2019. My God, help me to finish this process. One of the most negative side effects from the chemo treatment was numbness in my feet, which caused problems walking. I also experienced a lot of fatigue and was cold all the time. I prayed and asked God to cut the treatments in half. Because of these side effects, I was not able to be in the house of the Lord at times.

On May 17, 2019, my chemo doctor informed me that she may have to stop treatment because of the numbness in my feet. She had changed the dose of the medication for chemo twice already, but it did not stop the numbness. I had been praying that I would not have to do more than six treatments. Well, I had to do the twelve chemo treatments. The last treatment was August 14, 2019.

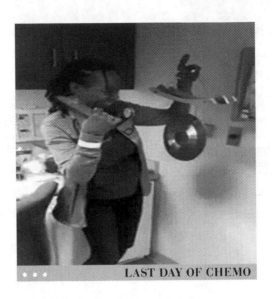

LAST DAY OF CHEMO

My healing process continued with the numbness subsiding some over the months. October came, and I was ready to go back to work—only to find out the job terminated me. They had my paperwork for a month before they let me go. I sent several emails before they finally responded. The response was to inform me of a scheduled phone call. The day before the call, while I was in worship, the Holy Spirit spoke and showed me what was going to happen on the call. The Spirit of God said, "They are going to let you go." He showed me the phone conversation taking place. The next day, I got the call, and it was just what the Holy Spirit gave me. I was not bothered by this because the Lord had spoken it in 2018, so I was mentally prepared.

He showed me that the person who was going to call me was going to sound genuinely nice and happy and then drop her bomb. Well, she did. I asked about a severance package. She replied with a no and stated that I had been receiving long-term disability. I said to her, "So that is what the company thinks of me? So you all are saying, 'Sorry for what happened to you, but have a good life'?" She hung up on me. Well, I went into prayer after that call on November 1, 2019. By November 15, 2019, God did it: he had them produce finances. I bless God for who he is in my life.

Now with no job, just as the Lord had said, I trust God to provide—and I must say, he has done just that. God has always been there for me during this time of my life. I stand on Matthew 6:33–34: "But seek ye first the kingdom of God, and his righteousness; and all these things shall be added unto you. Take therefore no thought for the morrow: for the morrow shall take thought for the things of itself. Sufficient unto the day is the evil thereof."

Going through this journey with the Lord has been an amazing experience. Yes, it was a turning point that I will never forget and the encounter with God that I am most appreciative of. So much revelation has come to light. I am reminded of Peter hearing the rooster's crow after he denied Jesus the third time. Peter remembered that Jesus had told him that he would deny Jesus three times.

6
CHAPTER

The End

I am coming up on a year after chemotherapy, and I give God all the glory for what he has done. My life has been rededicated to the Lord Jesus; it is because of him that I live, move, and have my being. I pray that my experience and testimony of the true and living God inspires someone to seek God. Whatever you might be going through, do not lean on your own understanding, but trust and acknowledge God in all that you do.

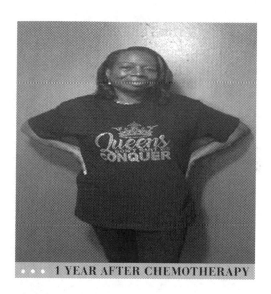

● ● ● **1 YEAR AFTER CHEMOTHERAPY**

Go in peace, and may you stand firm on our basic instructions from the Father before leaving earth.

Printed in the United States
By Bookmasters